Creative Talents Unleashed

I0201734

Presents

Love, A Four Letter Word

Love Poems From Around The World

GENERAL INFORMATION

LOVE, A FOUR LETTER WORD

1st Edition: 2014

This Publishing is protected under Copyright Law as a "Collection". All rights for all submissions are retained by the Individual Author and or Artist. No part of this Publishing may be Reproduced, Transferred in any manner without the prior **WRITTEN CONSENT** of the "Material Owner" or it's Representative Creative Talents Unleashed.

Publisher Information

Creative Talents Unleashed

www.ctupublishinggroup.com

1st Edition: Creative Talents Unleashed
CreativeTalentsUnleashed@aol.com

This Collection is protected under U.S. and International Copyright Laws

Copyright © 2014: Creative Talents Unleashed Authors

ISBN-13 : 978-0990500902 [Creative Talents Unleashed]
ISBN-10 : 099050090X

$13.95

Dedication

With loving hearts the poets featured in "Love, A Four Letter Word" donated their words of love for this publishing to help establish a starving artist fund for writers that may not be able to financially afford assistance in getting published. 100% of all proceeds from this book are being donated to the "Starving Artist Fund" to assist writers in becoming published authors.

We dedicate this book of love, to the unpublished authors that would love to be published.

Please visit our website for further details:

www.ctupublishinggroup.com/starving-artist-fund.html

Love: *Noun*

1. a profoundly tender, passionate affection for another person.
2. a feeling of warm personal attachment or deep affection, as for a parent, child, or friend.
3. sexual passion or desire.
4. a person toward whom love is felt; beloved person; sweetheart.
5. used in direct address as a term of endearment, affection, or the like

Definition by Dictionary.com

Table of Contents

Table of Contents... *Continued*

Table of Contents ... *Continued*

Table of Contents ... *Continued*

Table of Contents ... *Continued*

Epilogue

Meet our Poets

Table of Contents ... *Continued*

Table of Contents ... *Continued*

Love, A Four Letter Word

Love poems from around the world

FIRST LOVE

I remember the very first day I set my eyes upon you,
Hair in red pigtails & in a dress of pretty cornflower
blue,
Our first day at school & we were both so painfully shy,
Our desks together, I sweated so much, not knowing
why,
I lent you a soft pencil as you had forgotten yours at
home,
You smiled at me sweetly & shyly & I would inwardly
groan,
We became inseparable friends & I´d carry your heavy
old bag,
Summer vacations sped by & school days would so
often drag,
I´d hold your tiny hand & often steal a pure & chaste
little kiss,
We´d rush home to Gran´s cookies, something we´d
never miss,
We would fish & explore & we would muddy our
scuffed knees,
We would walk your small pup in the snow & not feel
the freeze,
The years flew by, we both grew up & we went our
separate ways,
Girlfriends came & went & then one day my new wife
came to stay,
I became a father & I heard that you had wed & too
became a mum,
The children arrived, grew & then their time came &
away they flew,

Love, A Four Letter Word

I am an old widower now, I´ve lived my life, but I´ve always loved you.

Sue Lobo

Deep Love

Sometimes I feel truly loved to the point of reading

every symbol in your mind.

I can communicate in telepathy with you.

Feed on your energy so positively and free.

I count on one finger the anomaly that is you.

I want to understand you but you are like a language

I am unfamiliar with.

Teach me. . .

 I want to learn you.

Who are you?

Where are you? I want to read you like an unread book.

Taste you like a cup of tea.

I want to dance with you in the moonlit sky.

I want to be in co-existence with you.

Are you willing to let me explore that inner you?

Stephanie Francis

I Miss You

With trepidation I remember those moments

When you took me in your arms for the first time,

Dizziness and stomach butterflies

When you kissed me first time my beloved

Today routine fills our lives,

Constantly on the run, no time for romance,

But I still miss you so much

And I hope that I will find you again one day.

Bozena Helena Mazur-Nowak

Man and Wife

For the eighteen years of my life,
Walk eighteen steps-
Towards me, my love!
As my Man and me your wife.
Although there was no red dress
Nor a ceremony!
But
There was love, lover and harmony!
Although there were no celebration,
No decoration
But
There was your smile and my elation.
Although there was no fabled art of collection,
But,
There were my eyes and your vision.
Although there was no crowd nor kinsmen,
But
There was the fire of love,
The blessing of GOD
The enchanting of azure winds
and our essence-embroiling
Penetrating, deep like the rays of the Sun!
To crown us for eternity.
For the eternal years of my life-
Walk with me, my love!
As my Man
and me your wife.

Disha Dinesh Sahni

5

'My Vain'

An unsung word
Which comes in my heart
Every time I breathe a half
Why you break my heart
Why you hate my heart
What about the oath you did take
What about your words of praise
What about the time we share
What about my cares
Oh dear
I want to hear
I want to hear
What was my mistake?
What wrong step did I take?
Its pain
Its pain
And it's my vain...

Mayank Nema

Love Letters

The genesis of innocence by happenstance
Timid in the approach; shall we dance
Time stood still in that moment
Consequences were to soon come; how to atone for it?
Years passed by with such regret
Sent out letters without a response yet
Depression from separation leading to a turbulent
tailspin
Oblivious to what was happening
Self-affliction becoming the new addiction
To curb the pain of a lost lover and friend
Searching for clues to no end
Too late it seems to begin anew
Moments of clarity embraced the tortured soul with a
beautiful view.

Lindsey Rhodes

We Were Non – Exist

Many words remain unsaid

How many tears on hold

Many glances we missed

How many paths we crossed

Many clouds rained

Many times we got drenched

But how many times we felt

Times, moments exist

But how many times we were non-exist

Jisha Viswanathan

Faded Memories

I fumble through old pictures

thinking and dreaming of you in moonlights past.

I wonder if you think of me the way I do you.

I can feel your absence lingering with me.

A faint memory of kissing you stays with me,

although you are no longer near.

I hate the fact that we do not co-exist in the same spaces.

Take me back into your arms where I felt the most comfort.

I want to feel safe again.

Stephanie Francis

Just-A-Break

I wish I could fake the thoughts
I wish I could tell how I feel
Seeking you...I find not
My fears are real now

I try to fake it but I can't hate it
I try to hate it but I still love it
What we shared, empty nights in the dark
What we dreamed - a life together

My heart bleeds
My eyes strains for sight of you
I see hope but its fate is fake
If love is fake, I'd be fake too

With a weary heart I sort for peace
Yeah...peace! Please!
What's of me in this den?
What's of me in this hell?

You are not gone - that's the faith I keep
You are gone - that's the belief I see
Forever? No! Just-a-break
That's the pain - just-a-break

Chiemezie Anyaeji Ugochukwu

Take Me to a Heart

Take me to a heart where true love and faithfulness exist
A heart that on hurting and betrayal it does never insist
take me to the heart where I can find true love
Where everything else is down but true love rise above
Take me to a heart where I can forget the pain I have
lived before
A heart that shields my pain and don't give me so much
more
Take me to the heart where I can fight away fears
Take me to the heart that wipes away my fears
Take me to a heart where love sets my soul free
A heart that I always find there for me
Take me to the heart that takes me by the hand
Makes me stronger and help again stand
Helps me live the beautiful life I had planned
Take me to the heart that fights away my pain
A heart whose love is not fake and in vain
Take me to the heart where I grand my love to possess
A heart that gives me love neither more nor less
Take me to the heart where true love is my cure
To the heart where I feel so safe and secure
Take me to the heart that turns my blindness into sight
A heart that turns my weakness into strength and might
Take me to the heart that hold me close and never let go
A heart has no place for anything but love to grow

Take me to the heart of love I had in mind
Is true love that so impossible to find

Mahinour Tawfik

A Sketch of the Eye

How do you describe a pair of beautiful eyes
At first thought everything has already been said
With clichés using every string of descriptive words
imaginable

When you really look at hers new thoughts rise up
Those eyes are artful, extraordinary and thrilling
Created from a masters pallet of shades of browns and
reds

Finer than the ultimate grades of mahogany or cocobolo
Textured and more complicated than burled walnut
Get a little closer, they begin to sparkle more than fine
gems

They pull you in beckoning instant attention
Step nearer where her breath is on your face
Not trying to focus on both, but on one then the other
So inviting and striking yet still very divergent
A sunburst of color igniting the iris flooded by echoes of
light

At first glance, unthinking, a pair of eyes seem identical
Not so, each is as diverse as the fingerprints of an entire
culture

Rusty Shuping

Rebound

If you are to stand in salt water with an open wound,
I will be right beside you. I do not possess
the sweetest of words; I will not praise all that you do.
But look around I will be there.
I am not capable of removing the hot rods strewn on
your path.
But I will definitely walk through your thorny bush up
until you.
You once called me a moon,
Please remember I wax and wane.
They say love is not love that finds change
I say, love is still love if it comes back.

Poovilangothai

Curiosity

She is Rose
A flower blossoming
Invites me to pluck
Its' blend of colors
Aroused my curiosity
To see
The lovely thing
Hidden inside

Sunil Algama

Three Years

It were three years of sweet memories
Three years of good moments
Captured none but by admiring eyes
It were three years of hugs and kisses
Three years of cuddling and wishes
Held not but by a loving man
It were three years of loving you
Three years of ambition and adoring you
Hoping against odds and ruin
It were great three years.

Three years of dream shattered
Three years of hearts broken
Three years of hope shaken
Three years of true love taken
Three years of paths deterred
Three years of sweetness tilted
 Three years of seemly wasted

But they are still three years memorable,
Of the best the world could offer, scalable
Engraved on minds walls un-detachable
Three years, I say three years

Ronald k Ssekajja

Barren No More

once a creek of bountiful flow
though lacking the dew the evening mist too
among the countless drying away

endured in abundance
snow-craving winters
rain-thirsty springs
long parched summers

yearning in solemn unease

a cloudburst then passed her impasse
through thick innumerable trees
amid myriads of blanketing streams
soaked one by one the bone-dry leaves

each of its caressing drop in gait
eased her drought of eternal wait

Hülya N. Yılmaz

Violin

You Say –
"The violin does not shed tears,
But sings melodious songs".

On the day of my return
From your native land
Leaving you alone
Prior to our separation
You took out your violin
And began to play.

Perhaps you wanted
To play better than before
To play the best ever
Perhaps,
About to be torn in two by time,
Incurably,
You wanted to forget
The impending wound of your heart and its pain.

However,
I was experiencing
The continuous sobbing of the violin
And, falling drop by drop
On my heart
The tears of your eyes.

You Say –

Love, A Four Letter Word

"The violin does not shed tears,
But sings melodious songs".

Bhisma Upreti

Translated by: Shashi Bhandary

Consent

Complete silence
I listened and listened
Terrible
I took a breath
Felt my heart beat
Abnormal
What's her reply?
Doubt
Lose forever
Ah!
She took my hand
Kissed
Place it on her heart
Murmured
I love you darling
The silence broke
And filled with laughter

Sunil Algama

Living Light

Another cool day with gloomy sky
The trees void of their leaves and color
She walks as if in a daze of loneliness
Eyes closed and peering through small slits
Afraid to open her eyes or just not enough strength
Looks toward her feet all around everywhere
The fire flies have come to cheer her
They will comfort her and guide her to warmth
Tiny miraculous insects that are so much taken for
granted
Get close and let the little living lights bump into you
They will make her feel alive again
With light comes love
After all, it does not stay cloudy forever

Rusty Shuping

Our Hearts Have Loved

And it was so clear, the long fingers pointing
The shadowy eyes from the dark, staring
And it was now clear, all she had said plainly
And it was painful how my guilt came to me daring
Those silent voices in my heart speaking
And there I stood, broken and regretting

I wished it had gone on well with her
That then our destinies would differ
But if the hand of time can't be turned back
Why then wouldn't my mind give me peace?
But haunt me still, even when I thought I meant well

Our lives are shaped, while eyes are faint
Our hands do write what our eyes have read
Our dreams do bring, what our eyes have seen
And our souls do long for what our hearts have loved

Ronald k Ssekajja

Immortal Love

I've been living in pain for so long
I've got no one, no where do I belong
I've never felt safe and never felt strong
You're the only person I wish to be among

I neither found the happiness nor could I pretend
I was left alone by myself with no brother or a friend
My heart was broken and no one cared to mend
I lived every moment begging this life to end

I don't know why this life has never been fair
It has been giving me too much to bear
It's filled me with grief sorrow and despair
It has left me no one who'd love and care

You gave me the happiness I've never known
you stood beside when I was left all alone
So much kindness and care you've shown
I no more have to face this life on my own

You erased the loneliness and emptiness inside
Everyone abandoned me, you stood by my side
Every time I lose my way, I find you there to guide
Your love is the only thing I never know how to hide

If words cannot tell, my eyes always reveal
The love and feelings my heart started to feel

Love, A Four Letter Word

I lived every lie but your love is the best real
Nothing but your love can get my wounds to heal

The past I lived, I never got to choose
You are the only one I wish never to lose
With you I lived the happiness I never knew before
I want to be with you, I ask for nothing more

I grant you my heart and soul to possess
I need your love nothing neither more nor less
As time passes your love grows in my heart
Binding us together even death can never part

Just promise that you won't cheat and betray
My love for you or you leave me alone some day
Or throw our painful memories so far away
And FORGET the life that WE lived yesterday

Mahinour Tawfik

Your Beauty

My piece of beauty,
Your beautiful face;
An irresistible charm
Your gorgeous body;
A mystery of creation,
So unique,
Giving me so much an of attraction,
And inflicting my mind with
So much of lovely thoughts.
Your beauty;
A perfection of God's creation,
The wonder and glamour of our time,
An irresistible gift of love,
The desire of every man,
And the dream of very creation.
Your beauty
Has adorned my
Every night dream,
And my imaginative thoughts.
Your beauty;
So total and natural,
Too desirable and attractive
Oh,
Please save me from this
State of lusting foolishly.

Okwor Maxwell Onyeka

Orange of the Departing Sun

Picturing an evening along with the mild rainfall,
Sun was illuminating the tiny drops
It rained some liquid gold. . .

I saw you coming to me,
My eyes were staring at your glory
Beach sand was glistening,
Sea was singing a mesmerizing
Song. . .

All of a sudden, as we came face to face,
Sea seemed to have become still,
Calm waves were giving a background melody of
romanticism;

Shore birds were humming the chorus
And our locked eyes started to perform
A Divine Duet
Note after note in rhythm....

I opened up my arms to give you the hug of solace,
My tears of joy were dying to tumble down and write
the tale of our pious love on your blank blushing face

My chest then became your eternal
Abode of tranquility,
My whispering voice, the pacifier
of your intimidated heartbeats .....

Our feelings got their wings
for a majestic flight over the heaven,

Love, A Four Letter Word

Sweetheart, what a soulful union it was

Emotions blended with our co-existence,
and Painted a riveting image of our
evergreen concord,
Which was watered down,
by the Orange of the Departing sun

Hrishikesh Padhye

Coffee Eyes

Morning rotation
Open eyes slowly
Mind rolls in from dreams
Thankful acknowledgement of being
Looking into the wisdom of her heart
I sip on those coffee eyes
A little cream with two sugars
for the right flavor
Deep, rich and brown color stirred up from the earth
Natural and rooted
Speaks wisdom without words
Calling out to me to come and embrace
And drink the morning look of love.....

Nolan P. Holloway, Jr

New Beginning

Greeted by a flirtatious grin
Assumed that the mind was closed but still admitted in
Introduced to a heart and world that was once cold
A beauty nevertheless to behold
Yearning for righteous attention but too afraid to express
Years of abuse, torment and mounting stress
Persistence while putting up a resistance and being
pursued
Fear inhabiting a weary soul; afraid of exploitation
A simple hello initiating the conversation
Platonic friendship materializing into something serious
Living in an insomniac's paradise to watch the sunrise
just to be curious

Lindsey Rhodes

Do You Love Me?

He climbs up my heart
Like creepers on windows
HE, who fills in me
Like rustling water into valleys
HE, whom the world may state as dark as the sky, when
the sun leaves
Is the brightest star in my life.
Invigorating my limbs...
Making my eyes coruscate
And Earth, Zion.
He, who is the inception of all ends
So atavistic, that no matter, I met him now...
The flavor is primordial
Yes! HE -
Comes close to my heart
And write softly on my palms-

'DO YOU LOVE ME?'

Disha Dinesh Sahni

Beyond Natural

It takes the brave to walk on broken bottles to the gate
of her heart . . .

Giants to gather courage before her presence
Philosophers to mend mirrors to reflect her image
Wise to take her cotton from fire
Rare humility to entertain her anger
Billionaires to buy her ring
Wisdom to understand her language
Utopian interpreter to understand her cry
Scribes to write her words
People with unequal minds to talk to her
Arch angels to sing her lullaby
Spiders to sow her garment

Warriors stand on top of mountains to call her
Cowards bow before her shadow from afar
Sincerity is the key to her gate
Perfect affection is the code to her room

She laughs with truthfulness
And frowns on betrayal
She knows no bounds to true heart

Zadok Kwame Gyesi

Not Yet

Cup of fragrant coffee is tempting and waiting
Aroma filled the room, I can feel the smell
My nose is growing like Pinocchio's nose

I do not want to get up I want to be with you,
You left your heart on the pillow next to me
I trapped you under my closed eyelids

I feel so good
Curtain dancing in the open window
I feel a gentle breeze on my neck

Trilling birds singing beautifully
Alarm clock brings me roughly to the ground
It's time to get up time for sparring with another day

Night my friend will
Bring you in my arms again

Bozena Helena Mazur-Nowak

Leaving it to fantasy

aching anew for his skin on mine
soft intense surprise-filled caress
yearning lips that never miss
the silkiest whisper of "yes?"
each time I utter his name

childlike smile in his eyes
in step with his handsome face
starting on those shapely feet
in invite to dance along with grace

wipes away my internal tears
appeases in faint promise to ease…

Hülya N. Yılmaz

The Meteor of Your Reality

You used to be my soulful nemesis,
Captivating me all in your dark eyes,
Never knew I was a victim of
delusion
Just a prey in the chamber of
Lies . . .

Like a sunlit water drop on a blade of
grass glistens its glory even more,
I believed you to be the flash of my
sword
never dreamed about being this
obscure . . .

I needed our tale to be painted by
the fabric of love , ending with the
colorful climax;
You made it a betrayal classic,
Left me as an utter Silent
Soundtrack . . .

Sheltering my exposed scars at this
stroke of time, my tears are writing
this life altering story;
In which, the disintegration of my
Life's planet was done by the

METEOR OF YOUR REALITY

Hrishikesh Padhye

33

Intimate Solitude

I want to be alone with you
Our circumstance rises above the lust that clouds the
worldly mind within a fog of confusion
To share the lovely loneliness with you for the
remaining days to serve our purpose
Not to just engage and live where everyone else stays
But seeking our own place
A commitment made to my chosen Beloved-forsaking
all others
As we move alone into the night-the consummate of
intimate light
Hard as steel but touches with the softness of silk
Transcending to an illuminating psyche
This intimacy is precious as we move with commitment
within our essence
I breathe your fragrance which brings me heat
Love flows to the tool of your desire.....will you join me
is this solitude?
We are one-and in love solitude
Daily being by ourselves to reflect and discover who we
are
I want to be alone
With you
As my Beloved Wife

Nolan P. Holloway, Jr

A Passionate Rendezvous

Two passionate lovers,
parted by the destiny of life
yearning for a rendezvous,
to get a glimpse of their love

At last, fortune smiled at them
ending the long awaited desire
both were together again
after long restless period of pain

It was a moment of mesmerizing delight
a longed tryst in his abode on a dark new moon night
like lustful lovers they osculated each other in shower
unleashed the fountain of sensual power

Drunk with the nectar of youthful essence
they became raw in each other's presence
tardily moving his lips on her bod
he became instantly her pleasure God.

She reclined defenseless on the bed,
inviting her beloved to be the head
gleefully accepting the invite,
he moved close, to hold her tight

Her curvaceous body appealed him
she flaunted her bosom to evoke his whim
her long dark hair spread over his chest
she bosomed his lustful lips to her breast

35

Like two entwined mating Serpents
exploring deepest pleasures of love
their bare bodies immersed in congress
relishing the ecstatic moment of their life

Their unabated hedonic delights
aroused them to new orgasmic heights
Their bodies melted in each other,
on that freezing dark night.

Sreejith Kulaparambil

How I Vision You

I.

Can I swim through your ripples
of cleansing azure
Stand up to your tempest?
Wash up on your shore?
Embrace the polarity
of your allure?
Can I try on your silhouette
like a lost contour?

II.

Your skin is a breeze
and my hands want to fly
My fingers are wings
in the flesh of your sky
You're stars and I'm stripes
on the peak of July
when your dunk tank ripples
suck my fireworks dry

III.

Tell me that I'm overboard
or that I'm not too bright
It gives me further reason
to seek out your guiding light
I may not be a poet

but these lover's words are true
Flawed only in your flawlessness
That's how I vision you

Steven Fortune

Shores of Love

He took
my world
by storm
when he
crashed
upon the
shores of my life
Enchanting my soul
flooding my heart
with his love
passionately
swimming in the sea
our love
forever
entwined
surviving
all
time

Gracey Flynn

My Fantasy

Every night you come in my dream
Flowing through my mind and body like a rampant
stream
I thirstily wait for your presence
Like the droughty land waits,
For the first rain drop of monsoon
You dawn into my life like a fresh breeze of wild love
Yet your serene beauty and face resembles a dove
You tickle my dormant sensation
And make me wild with passion
Where are you my beloved?
I am yearning for your presence
Oh! I always wished you be there beside me
To make my life a sultrily glee
I would hold you tight in my arms and dance
And make love with you in the dark rainy nights
kissing your forehead, and coming down to your cheek
I want to osculate every part of yours in streak
my wet lips long for those warm bosoms
and my arms eager to wrap your waist
I wish to hear your sensuous voice
When our body swings wild without poise
Our vital vigor's would rise to orgasmic heights
Then our souls would become one and blissfully light
In those lighter and ecstatic moments of love
I wish you cuddle me like a mother caring her child
And I blissfully sleep on your warm tender thighs.

Sreejith Kulaparambil

Lord of My Love

They have seized me from loving
But they have failed to stop my heart beating
And this bag of flesh they let be
I shall use to obey my love for thee
I shall love thee even in my grave

Seize me not to speak
Thy love is my life
Hereby this window time strolls fast
Leaving me behind to sink in affection

Dethroned to passion O' my position
May I be dead not see thy face again
But may I live to love thou again
King of my heart
Ruler of my heart
Rule me to love thee greater than these
Loyal to face thou command my breeze
Lodging nostril knower of mine
Sanctioned of love, governed by mine
Before our love be tested to die
Pass me thy hand softly; how

I define love before thou
As thy specious spirit of my past
Dwelling in the flesh of her man
Traced from the eye's only shy
Traced from the heart beating fast
Traced from the "yes" of the mouth
And I call thou the goddess . . .
Who skimmed the moon of my love

Love, A Four Letter Word

The one who taxed me to love her less
Of her beauty ridden' horse
The lady of my life
The keeper of my heart

Robert Ebi

Love Mathematics

Before me is a sum
And the mathematics is on my shoulder
Minus, minus, plus, minus, minus, plus
is the formulae.

How do you win the heart of a virgin girl?
All you have to do is sing a love anthem
and recite the pledge
Thus it goes

If you find her romantic eye's skipping
Your eye's, find a rose.
And when your rose find out she wears a heart
be sure there is a kind of man she likes.

Maybe he's the kind who sings like a Nightingale
and calls her name in every rhyme
Maybe he's the kind who smiles all time
and sweet in touch as a hive.

Maybe he's the kind who plays on shores
and have her not to every chores
Maybe he's the kind who's worthy of trust
and mindful of breasts and not.

So is the sum
If she is one, and you are one, find her not
If she is tough and you are rough, rush her not . . .
Sure, if I can sing

To call her name in every rhyme
to smile with her
all the time as her kind
I am sure. I am that very man

Robert Ebi

You Affect Me

Magnetic eyes
Magical pulls
Under a spell . . .

Pulse gone wild
Hormones on rampage
I am seized . . .

Captivating chemistry
Sizzling desires
Existence stirred . . .

Pulsating rhythms
Throbbing my head
Calling your name . . .

Coaxing longings
Whisper gently
Take up the journey . . .

Girish Sangle

Making Sense

Eyes believing themselves
Ears believing other people
Intuition believing the truth of spirit.

My senses awakened at last . . .

My eyes falling for the sight of you
My ears liking all that you say
Intuition guiding me along the way.

You take me beyond my senses. . .

Inhaling your sweet aroma
Touching your soft, smooth skin
Tasting your lips gently placed upon mine.

 Intertwined senses, yours and mine.

Raja Williams

Special Words

There is special words,
That we like to hear.
Words with great hope,
Words that bring cheer.
It's something we need,
Through each passing day.
When we are unhappy,
They show a new way.
The words that I need,
Are from a small mind.
She hasn't seen life,
But yet she's so kind.
Sometimes what she says,
Can make me feel glad,
The words she says best;
I love you my dad.

Tony Roberts

Friendship

In life we find someone,
That we call a friend.
Conversation comes easy,
From beginning to end.
The moment we meet them,
And look in their eyes.
Something special has happened,
What a great surprise!
We want to be near them,
And give them so much.
To get only closer,
As if we're their crutch.
Tomorrow seems easy,
Just knowing they're near.
Looking forward to sharing,
All of their cheer.
This one special person,
Is so hard to find.
It's like walking in darkness,
Without being blind.
I want you to know,
Our love is so true.
You'll always be special;
I'll always love you!

Tony Roberts

Its Name is Simple

Like a chirp of the bird in the woods
Like the croak of the frog in the creek
Like the moon illuminates the universe
Like the hunter in the field searching fools to eliminate
Like the lion in the jungle seeking permission to devour

At the feel of it, the heart tingles
At the touch of it, the body smiles
At the sip of it, the mind blows
At the sense of it, who can stand?
Whichever way, its peace to some and pain to another

It controls the very sense of human
King's kill to keep it, slaves die to keep it
Its wave is incontestable
Its force smiles at gravity, laughs at the sun
Whichever way, you will need a miracle

Its sweet, its soar
Gets the bittered to smile
Gets the cripples to dance
Gets the dumb to speak
Yeah...it's that unique!

You fell it, you see it
Its experienced, not taught

Love, A Four Letter Word

A feel can elevate a heart
A touch can change a life
Its name is simple

It's Love

Chiemezie Anyaeji Ugochukwu

Knocking of Love

Drink the fragrance
Taste the beats
Unfollow the rhythm
Just follow your heart
You won't understand what is it?
It is the knocking of love.

Mayank Nema

Many Voices

I struggled within the powers of doubt
To see my uncovered shyness
Opened to the eyes of the chosen one
I faced the realities of truth
Which has been verified with time
In the world of humanity

I melted within her hands
Pressing down my sweat on her laid sheet
Under the cover of darkness
When the night diffused
Voices of tarantulas
To the itchy ears

I danced to her screaming tunes
When I coiled to her magical touches
Under her velvet
To block the beaming rays
From hitting on our uncovered skins

She led me into a fountain
Where million have drunk from it
And left me alone on its banks
With a broken cup

I looked around to see where she passed
But I could not see the traces of her footprints . . .
On the soil of ancient land
I bruised my heart in agony
Wondering on the path to go

Love, A Four Letter Word

Till I heard the still voice of her waters
Falling from the cliffs of her fountain

Zadok Kwame Gyesi

Whispers in the Morning

I like these, our whispers in the morning
I love the look in your grey eyes
Snuggle up to you baby
I feel your every move every tremor
Your voice is warm and mild
I cannot give up this love

You and I were meant to be I know it
You give me your warm hand
I'm so happy in your arms
All this brutal world disappears somewhere
Sometimes it looks like I'm far away
Do not worry baby I'm next to you

Chasing something I do not know
Sometimes a little scared but I'm
With you in the name of our love
Ready for a journey into the unknown with you
The beating of your heart calms me
Doubt disappears in the blink of an eye

I love these our whispers in the morning
I love you

Bozena Helena Mazur-Nowak

Intimate Moments

My fingers slid through his.

Tangled and twisted in a loving embrace.

I love you, I love you, I love you,

You say reassuring me of your heart's content.

Longing for your touch, anxious for the warmth of you.

I love you.

You speak to me so clearly and vividly.

I know the truth of your heart.

The caress of your soul.

The vibration of your energy.

The realness that is you.

Stephanie Francis

Love Story

At first it was thought true love doesn't exist
But in front of true love, the hearts cannot resist
The day they met their lives have begun
Every moment they lived before, was gone
The first real smile on their faces was drawn
Real happiness in their heart has grown

They tried too much to hide
The love the passion they hold deep inside
Words weren't said but their eyes did reveal
the love the passion their hearts would always feel

He was everything she has ever longed for
She gave him true love he has never felt before
One day he surprised her and so loudly he confessed
That his heart and soul only she possessed

She promised to stay forever by his side
Make him happy warm and satisfied
He promised to hold on to her and never let go
In happiness forever they shall grow

In his arms she could feel so safe and secure
From all his pain she was his cure
Through her blindness he was her sight
Through his darkness she was his light

They lived in bliss joy and laughter
They lived in happiness every moment ever after

Mahinour Tawfik

Affirmation of a New Love

Words that have Life
In a place I have never been
Inside me to express to your heart
With someone I feel I've known for some time
Verbalization through My Spirit and Body

Movement in moments
I so love You -My world is metaphoric
Conversations deep and rooted in the Sprit
Everything speaks to me in the language of Your love
What sprang from the soil was a new flower
Our natures whisper through infinite moments-
Pollinated with inner searching and mutual love
Expanding and contracting simultaneously
Can one explain nature and its inner workings?

Guiding Me
Science can only probe so far
To be in your presence
I chose to ride on faith and believe in us
Hearing your verbal vibrations quivers my soul
Makes me feel life plugged in earth's socket
My eyes behold Your essence that can quench My thirst
My creative side pulses with unbounded energy
Overflowed
Shocks inner self to breathe because for a moment I
forgot
Intentions of wanting to embrace Your mind
We both share in the newness of an old feeling we have
had with others

Love, A Four Letter Word

The Spirit of
this journey has started in a moment of realization
That is who You are
Something different being enthused . . .

Went into myself to find You
Basking in unknown, unfettered and pure
Now I am joined to your life

Not tainted by past memories or feelings
This Journey
Not dragging life's baggage
On a noble quest
Free to discover, ravage and revel in what we have
defined
To find purity from filthiness
Perfection from flawed desires
Need you to grow me

To be a better Man
Your Man
As New Love
Affirmed and dedicated to You

Nolan P. Holloway, Jr.

Counting Sand

All the sand of the world might be counted
One grain at a time, how long would it take
Even with the new sand created each day
Counting and counting
Once done it would only begin eternity
Put every speck of the earth's sand in one giant glass
Each huge glass full is only one speck compared to
eternity
That would only be a small beginning
So it is with the Love of God

Rusty Shuping

When You Smile

You kill me when you smile
With those lips
It's like the sky just lightened up
And that glitter from your eyes
Oh my

There's something about your voice
When you call me honey
You leave me with no choice
But to give my heart to you only

Your smile washed away the stains of guilt and shame
Wound and pain
Deeply rooted within
You have restored hope and confidence in my once
hopeless heart

You glued together my once broken heart
Oh love
You are the love I've been waiting to love
The hope I once hoped for

You touched my past away
To the highly anticipated future ahead
I surrender my all to love
Only love defined by your eyes . . .

I give you my all
Unto your hands
I handover my heart

Love, A Four Letter Word

Take it with you
So wherever you go
Wherever you are
My heart will always be with you

There's no minute that passes without
me thinking of you
You make my blood boil
Your skin so smooth like oil
Rubbing against mine
I like the way you make love to me.

Siphumle Botya

When Love Met Love

When love met love
When one heart met the other
When my eyes found comfort in your smile
When I realized that I had found thee that my mind
knew not of
When everything including the world's turn took a pause
When love had finally found love

When that feeling had conquered your body
Mind and soul gave in to the weakness of the heart
When time finally told it was time
When the heart felt it was right to love the love that love

When I looked around
And realized my feet were off the ground
Wings I had found
To fly away to a place beyond the clouds
A place where love could love me proud

When love found me scared and hurt
When love saved my soul from the hatred that had
become of the word
When not anymore did I have to endure the bitterness of
the world

When a second chance was granted to this that was once
an undeserving heart . . .

Love, A Four Letter Word

When love met love
When one heart met the other
They continued to beat in one beat
One rhythm, rhythm of love

Siphumle Botya

Your Email

I received your email today,
And with it a delicate fragrance
And humble affection;
And, pervading the whole message,
A lovely feeling –
Warm, so warm –
Pleasant, oh how pleasant:
I received an appetite for life.

This evening
And the oncoming night,
Of all nights, they're mine,
So beautiful.
I want to hold them to myself,
Pulling them around me.

Wrapped as under a quilt,
In my feelings,
I will sleep soundly tonight,
And dream.

I received your email today.

Bhisma Upreti

Translated by: Shashi Bhandary

Without Him

If I did not have him
I would have
No light,
No smile,
No reason to laugh,

No sunshine,
No moon,
No shining stars,

No joy,
No love,
No life,

Just sadness,
and bitterness,
Just darkness,
and emptiness,

For he is the breath
of my soul
without him
I would wither
and grow cold

Gracey Flynn

Lying Close to You

Oh my love,
The nights shared with you
Have remained so memorable in my mind,
Nights when I will
Lay very close to you,
Our arms holding each other tightly,
Our warm breathe
Soothing our lips,
Rekindling our love and
Affection for each other.
The memories of those nights
Have often brought smiles on my face,
Inflicting my mind with gladness;
Such that nourishes my soul.
And while I am away,
I keep thinking of
When I will be back to home,
To share my nights with you,
To savor your warm arms and breath
Lying so close to you
Has made my nights so beautiful,
And it makes my heart glad
knowing that I will always wake up
To look at your beautiful face
And smile happily.

Okwor Maxwell Onyeka

Silent Night

Silent night,
Shining bright
All for love,
Sent from above
The Savior did come our sins to erase.
Killed by cruel hands on this earthly base,
His love didn't wane nor falter
Nor did the pain his weakness flatter
But He endured for Love's sake
That we'd be new
Like the dew,
That comes every day break.

Covenant Chimnonso

Love's Tree

We all find a love,
That we really need.
We give it new life,
And plant a new seed.
As this love grows,
There's so much to see.
This new little seed,
Starts a beautiful tree.
Our heart feels great changes,
From love we have found.
Our roots are now growing,
They spread underground.
Our trunks will grow up,
And limbs will grow out.
The life our seed got,
Is now very stout.
Sometimes this love fades,
And we don't see the reason.
Now we lose leaves,
Like changing of season.
We have to decide,
What tomorrow will bring.
Will our seed stay strong,
Will we have a new spring.
Some of us choose,
To let it pass by.
This seed that was special;
Will now have to die.

Tony Roberts

Amplified Love

My soul knows the truth . . .

Love is everywhere I look
In every person
And every situation

Amplified love will
Wake even the buried
Absent and hidden

Difficult situations contain the seeds of love
They are waiting to emerge
To awaken the dormant heart

Dead layers peeling off and shedding
Awoken by the beating heart
Beat by beat love begins to emanate once again

Let your soul amplify
And light up the love that lies within you
Like the brightest star in the sky

Acknowledge all the love
Compassion and kindness
You already express and embody

Feel the soul love flowing within you
Let the divine light pour out of you
And the seeds planted will grow

Love, A Four Letter Word

Amplify love, and you will increase it.

Raja Williams

My True Feeling

My love,
You may not posses
The divine gift of beauty,
That may be shining
So bright like the morning sun,
So attractive like the rose flower.
I may have been
Taken for being foolish
For falling deep in love with you.
People may have passed their
Judgment against you;
Simply referring to you
As not good enough.
But,
In loving you,
I have been blind,
I have looked
Beyond your face,
To look deep into your heart,
Where your true beauty lies,
Where our love shares together,
Where our feelings are felt,
Deeper than human thoughts.

Okwor Maxwell Onyeka

Intersection

My road has stopped
at the intersection you changed

Your way…
with no motivation
to find new paths

I abandon my journey here…

I have emptied
all the ironies of Life
in to the abyss of fate…

Now I just want to
rest here
and think about you warmly…

Till my soul
finds a new body…

Girish Sangle

Breaking Free

Gone were the enchantment and the mystique
Standing out in the crowd that made her unique
Cannot find the words for her to express
The emotions instilled in the young soul caused by the
stress

Mentally trying to right the wrongs
An outcast from the rest of the world; thinking on how
she belongs

Until she was greeted with a kindred spirit
Wanting to alter her course but too afraid to come near it
After much persistence she embraced the light
Determined to move forward without giving up the fight

Lindsey Rhodes

Addicted to Love

Obligations surrendered to our
Narcotic need for
Ecstasy

Needing to feel love's kiss
I turn to you in my emptiness
Grasping to
Hold love's sweetness
Tending to desires call...

Skin to skin
Touching my chest
Ambitions let go to
Nourish the need
Damned if I do . . .

Act upon such a deed, a one-night stand is not what I
need.

Raja Williams

Desperation

Lost words to define a beauty
Caught in desperation and desire
Such a smile I desire to my heart
My thoughts I fake not again
For a smile I desire
To debug my fears
Please shelter my insecurity
I crave for safety in your arms

Expressions is beyond me
A weakness that holds me bound
For I die to say it
I wish to live to see it
Argue not my inconsistency
It's only found in this quest
A quest am prepare to die
To die in Silence

I see hope in my pen
Understanding in your heart
That is my strength
To pen 'I Need You'
Your voice keeps me mute
Your beauty fakes my thought
Your character my mama desire
Obi m! I love you

Chiemezie Anyaeji Ugochukwu

Roses in the Soil

Shy me not in the face of the world
Don't shun me like how yesterday's sun died
out in the darkness for today's fame
Submerge me under the canopy of your true heart
Fan the embers of fidelity in our love
Follow my footsteps of faithfulness in truth
Shower me with joy
And drench me with living happiness
Show me the entrance of peace
And walk me out through the exit door of amusement
Let the flavor of your love shine in the skies
Like the appearing sun licking the face of the ocean
Drink deep or taste not the true reflection of my love
Embraced me with the claws of understanding
And kissed me with tenderness
From infinitive fountains of your love
Have I yeaned the quenching movement of your love?

Zadok Kwame Gyesi

Canopy of Blue Sky

Canopy of blue sky
Matching my dress
Dancing on ocean
Waves matching my steps
my waist in his strong hands
I swirl, swirl
I will not fall I'm sure
Everything around us is unknown
Whose sky, whose sea
Only known to us is this moment
Moment with emotion deeper like ocean
our eyes moved along with our steps
Every move expressed the love, where our lips remained
silent
The universe too conspired to move
to direction where heart is
towards love that is eternal

Jisha Viswanathan

Fictive Mind

last night sleepless for my rare trip to a vacation
a popular television show attracted my full attention
a woman falls in love with a man: a couple quite becoming
his news reaches her before no return:
ex-girlfriend is expecting
he confesses in grave anguish
he must stand by the mother of his baby
five months for both are still ahead...maybe...
the inescapable force of all forces falls upon her
Eros had long ago chosen him for a custom-cast spell
"my heart will get broken," she knows –
"what if, though, it is all worth it?"

today on the road Sezen offered me her Turkish soul song
"I couldn't know I would hurt you by loving you so"
the agony of her love destined to be a no go

expectant and fulfilled arrival at my breathing space
I did not travel light for a three night room and board
put to shame the record of my ten-day case for abroad

my first night out
I put on a black sleeveless midi dress
threw over a blood orange whole-body shawl
heavy glimmer jewelry accompanied to impress
black open-toe shoes high-heeled quite décolleté
may have been in vain for a woman dining alone
as far as the judgments would wonder in stress
this soul ascertained to tell itself a different tale

78

it was there with you donning a smile of enormous scale
with each of the slow sips
its unending delectable wine
its mind dove deeper to a smooth rain-washed lake,
rather divine
it then devoured the immaculate sunset for two
before its inventive eyes

oh, by the way, it wasn't all black or blood orange on me

there too was something bright red inside...
my bleeding heart

Hülya N. Yılmaz

Soul to Soul

Inhale me

Breath as one

Let us exhale our barriers

Take me beyond rights & wrongs

Dive into deep

Ripple the stillness

Let us make union whole

Soul to Soul

Jisha Viswanathan

Another Soul

This story tells a story of a soul that have let go of
another soul
If it was an ordinary fiery tale I'd begin by saying once
upon a time

But it speaks of an extraordinary pain that no word can
explain
A pain that have claimed a person's name he is now
called lame
Lonely melodies evoked enclosed memories
Tears having been shed
Time flew as if it was sped

It was only yesterday that my time I spent
Unconscious minded that this day I'll crave your smile
My heart breaks as I wave good bye

Call me a sun
Call me a moon
Call me mountains and rivers
I need believers who'll believe and deliver this feeling to
nations my emotions
can't reach

I need to teach and preach the precautions of love loving
a loveless lover
The danger of anger when a stranger invades your heart
And cut off your gut to stand your ground

They say its love and it's blind

Love, A Four Letter Word

But it feels like a knife stabbing me from behind
It's no joke
My heart is broken
I guess louder my silence spoke
Of a story that provoked the way I see myself.

Siphumle Botya

My Desire

My desire
Is to hold you before my eyes...

This world is
Not worth seeing at present –
Blood and bloodstains everywhere
Terror, and more terror everywhere
Haharardous running, and
Uncertainty everywhere
I am disgusted
With constantly seeing,
Hearing,
Facing all of this
Every day, and every night.

When you are with me
Uncertainty and terror vanish
Faith in life soars to its pear
And under the clear blue sky
Desires take flight
On the colourful wings
of the will to live.

This world is
Not worth living at present,
I wish to experience it with you at my side
I wish to see it through your eyes . . .

O my sacred love!

Love, A Four Letter Word

My desire
Is to hold you before my eyes....

Bhisma Upreti

Translated by: Shashi Bhandary

EUPHORIA

Lie within my arms & dream of starry skies,
Let me bury my face in your hair,
Let my lips brush your neck,
Kissing your breasts & heavy lidded eyes,
EUPHORIA.

Close your eyes & feel my touch,
Skin of soft velvet cream,
Feel the hot exotic dream,
Of my loving you so much,
EUPHORIA.

Hair of twisted spun flame,
Splayed upon your pillow,
Entwined with love's willowed whispers,
That knows no wilting sorry shame,
EUPHORIA.

Briny tears dripping whole,
Do not weep with sorrow,
Ride the foam of reason,
As I enter your eternal soul,
EUPHORIA.

Sue Lobo

Harmonic Souls

The
orchestra
played
never
skipping
a note
A perfect
unison
of harmony
spoke
with
a
whisper
and a
touch
a melody
of our
souls
began to
sing
 of a
wondrous
love
together
our souls
forever
shall
bring

Gracey Flynn

Your Face

Its hard to explain
but one just gets drawn to a Face
the way I do…when I look at you…

Your Eyes…Your Hair…
the way you stand and
look at the Camera…

I sense a flicker within
My Heart goes warm
and my soul gently glows…

You are distant
away…unattainable…
Yet so close

I can see the walls
You have built around
to keep me away…

Shall I hammer them down
or gently wait For them
to crumble on their own…

Shall I walk all the distance
or wait for you too…
to walk few miles towards me…

I remain engulfed…
in these sweet uncertainties'
day after day…

But certainly
I wont ever let this liking
for your Face Die...

Girish Sangle

Passing Through

I was beginning to believe
I was destined to
walk in the land of loneliness

Until one day a powerful
force walked right
on through me…

This feeling I
can't quiet describe,
what am I feeling inside?

A thump, thump
up in my chest,
a feeling unknown
I must confess

Looking down
I can see,
she walked
right on through me…

Is this how it is
to give and take,
connections made

Love, A Four Letter Word

on a leap of faith?

Or is this just
a simplified case
of passing through
and thinking, it might be you?

Wanting to share my open-heart space.

Raja Williams

Epilogue

Creative Talents Unleashed

Inspiration Starts Here

Creative Talents Unleashed

Creative Talents Unleashed is a publishing group that offers an inspiring platform for both new and seasoned writers to tap into and participate in. We offer daily writing prompts and challenges to fuel the writer's mind, a variety of writing tips, and much more. We are honored to assist writers expand and grow in the journey of becoming published authors.

For More Information

Creative Talents Unleashed

Creativetalentsunleashed@aol.com

www.ctupublishinggroup.com

Creative Talents Unleashed

Our Links

Website

www.ctupublishinggroup.com

Blog

www.creativetalentsunleashed.com

Facebook

www.facebook.com/creativetalentsunleashed

Twitter

https://twitter.com/CTUPublishing

Tumbler

http://creativetalentsunleashed.tumblr.com/

Pinterest

https://www.pinterest.com/creativetalents/

Instagram

https://instagram.com/ctupublishinggroup/

Writing Groups

www.facebook.com/groups/WritersConnection

www.facebook.com/groups/ctupublishing

Meet Our Poets

Creative Talents Unleashed

Creative Talents Unleashed

www.ctupublishinggroup.com

Introducing Bhisma Upreti

Born in Jhapa, Nepal, Bhisma Upreti has published 6 books of poetry and 8 books of essays. His works have been translated into English, Korean, Japanese, German, Serbian, Slovenian and Hindi. His works have appeared in many literary journals and anthologies including Grey Sparrow, The Enthusiast, PEN Point, Our Voices, Indo-Asian Literature, The Art of Being Human, The Skeleton, Lost Coast Review, Aan Harbour and other Nepali Literary Journals and magazines. He is the recipient of First prize in National Poetry Festival organized by Nepal Academy of Literature. He is a joint secretary of Nepal Chapter of PEN International.

Upreti got his Masters degree in Economics from the University of Southampton, UK. Upreti lives in Kathmandu with his family and works at Central Bank of Nepal.

Bhisma can be reached at:

Email: bhisma.upreti@gmail.com

Love, A Four Letter Word Contributions:

Introducing Bozena Helena Mazur-Nowak

Bozena Helena Mazur-Nowak was born in 1958 and comes from Opole (Poland). In search of work she migrated to the UK. She lives in Merstham near London. Her poems were published on web portals. Many work of the poet can be found on her Facebook profile. Bozena Helena's literary debut was the line "our love" (2011), which won first place in the competition of one line. This poem and many others, was published in the pages of The Polish Observer, Angora. The poet has released three volumes of poetry in Polish. The first "on the banks of the river called life" in 2011, the second "ticket to the Happiness station" in 2012, the third "on the departure bridge" in 2013.

Bozena can be reached at:

www.facebook.com/bozenahelenam

Email: bozena.mazur-nowak@hotmail.co.uk

Love, A Four Letter Word Contributions:

Introducing Chiemezie Anyaeji Ugochukwu

Chiemezie U. Anyaeji is Writer, Leadership Strategist, Educationist and a Building Technologist. He writes on a broad range of subjects for Humanity and to free the Mind. Graduate of Building Technology. His works has been published in the No 1 Online Media in Nigeria, Abuja Media, journals, and magazines. He was the Editor of the Trumpeter, University of Abuja, Nigeria. He has lead numerous Editorial Teams. He writes for leisure. He continues to grow his passion for the Africa Project.
Data Analyst with MTN Nigeria.
He lives in Delta, Nigeria.

Chiemezie can be reached at:

www.seedwrites.wordpress.com

Love, A Four Letter Word Contributions:

Introducing Covenant Chimnonso

Covenant Chimnonso, also known as Nonsopoet Chimnonso is a Nigerian budding poet who believes in the power of the pen.

Covenant can be reached at:

www.facebook.com/covenant.chimnonso1

http://nonsothoughts.wordpress.com/

Email: nonsopoetic@gmail.com

Love, A Four Letter Word Contributions:

Introducing Disha Dinesh Sahni

I am Disha Dinesh Sahni from Jabalpur, Madhya Pradesh, India. I am pursuing engineering in industrial and production from Jabalpur engineering college. I have been publishing my works in various magazines and newspaper in India and abroad. I am also a member of Keynotes poets and writers in Sacramento, California.

Love, A Four Letter Word Contributions:

Introducing Girish Sangle

Girish is a Mechanical Engineer, working as a Sr. Manager-Purchase in a Engineering Projects Construction Company in South India.

Reading is a hobby and he has a deep interest in literature, writing, reading, and Poetry is a Passion.

Love, A Four Letter Word Contributions:

~ Gracey Flynn ~

Introducing Gracey Flynn

As a young child I put a pen in my hand and felt the passion fill my soul as my words came to life through poetry. Sharing my faith and my love for my Creator through my words is my greatest reward.

Gracey has also contributed her work to "I Am Poetry"

http://www.bookrix.com/_ebook-various-poets-i-am-poetry/

Love, A Four Letter Word Contributions:

Introducing Hrishikesh Padhye

My name is Hrishikesh Padhye. I am from India. I am a 20 year old male pursuing a bachelor of engineering degree here in India from the Civil engineering branch. I love creativity and creative minds and I am passionate about writing. I love to learn different languages.

Hrishikesh can be reached at:

https://www.facebook.com/hSpadhyE

Love, A Four Letter Word Contributions:

Introducing Hülya N. Yılmaz

Hülya N. Yılmaz, a college professor in Liberal Arts, authored a book on Rumi's ghazals (a.k.a. love poetry) and their influence on 19th and 20th century German literature. She contributed a chapter to a scholarly work on the 2006 recipient of the Nobel Prize for Literature, Orhan Pamuk. Her tri-lingual poetry appears in Trance, published 2014 by Inner Child Press, ltd. At the present time, she teaches in her fields of specialty; continues with her creative writing; is a self-appointed literary translator and a novice free-lance writer.

Hülya can be reached at:

https://www.facebook.com/NHulyaY

http://dolunaylaben.wordpress.com

Her book Trance can be found at:
http://www.innerchildpress.com/h%C3%BClya-n-yilmaz.php

Love, A Four Letter Word Contributions:

Introducing Jisha Viswanathan

Jisha Viswanathan a poet from India, loves reading, and writing poetry. He started writing from a young age and has poems published in two anthologies.

Jisha can be reached at:

www.facebook.com/jisha.viswanathan

Love, A Four Letter Word Contributions:

Introducing Lindsey Rhodes

Lindsey Rhodes is an inspiring poet who is currently an administrator of The Writers' Connection group. As a former military veteran; he sought to writing as an outlet to deal with the rigmarole. He is also a part of many writing groups on various social media outlets. He is originally from New Orleans but now resides in Ohio with his girlfriend and his two children.

Lindsey can be reached at:

https://www.facebook.com/lf.rhodesii

https://www.facebook.com/groups/WritersConnection/

Love, A Four Letter Word Contributions:

Breaking Free   73

Love Letters   7

New Beginning   28

Introducing Mahinour Tawfik

Mahinour Tawfik is a 20 year old from Egypt. She is a medical student born into a family of pharmacists. She wants to be a psychiatrist. Her hobbies are poetry and listening to songs and participation in charity work. Her dream is to travel around the world and be a well-known poetess and a successful psychiatrist.

Mahinour can be reached at:

https://www.facebook.com/mahinour.tawfik

Love, A Four Letter Word Contributions:

Introducing Mayank Nema

Mayank Nema is pursuing Information Technology engineering from Jabalpur Engineering College, Jabalpur, Madhya Pradesh, India. I am the junior editor of our college magazine. And am also currently working with one social called Kaarwaa.N. Aiming social welfare.

Love, A Four Letter Word Contributions:

Introducing Nolan P. Holloway, Jr.

Nolan has been writing poetry for over three years now. He is originally from Queens NY. He truly enjoys sharing his experiences through poetry.

"I have truly found my voice." ~ Nolan P. Holloway, Jr.

Nolan can be reached at:

https://www.facebook.com/npholloway

http://nhollowayscribe.wix.com/nolan-holloway

Love, A Four Letter Word Contributions:

Introducing Okwor Maxwell Onyeka

I am Okwor Maxwell, born on the 16th day of November 1992. A Nigerian of enugu state origin. I am an under graduate of building technology, I became a published author in 2013 for my play 'vengeance of the spirit' by Rasmed publications Ibadan. I am a book promoter and reviewer at http://worldsbestbooks.net/

Okwor can be reached at:

https://www.facebook.com/maxwellbillions

Love, A Four Letter Word Contributions:

Introducing Poovilangothai

Very rarely in life people get to get to follow their passion in their profession. Literature is my passion and profession. I am an Assistant Professor of English in Bhaktavatsalam Memorial College for Women, Chennai. The search for meaning of literary pieces led to a search for the self. After a decade long relationship with literature, I am proud to recognize myself with my spiritual and physical self – a whimsical, uncompromising woman

Poovilangothai can be reached at:

http://poovilangothai.wordpress.com/

Love, A Four Letter Word Contributions:

Rebound   **13**

Introducing Raja Williams

I am Raja, a free spirited American woman with a name from India that means king. I walk the path of spirituality connecting with people, animals and nature. My insights are shared through my poetry and thoughts. I am the author of "The Journey Along The Way", a book of poetic insights published in 2013. I am the Founder of the publishing group Creative Talents Unleashed.

Raja can be reached at:

Email: Rajasinsight@aol.com

Web: www.Rajasinsight.com

www.facebook.com/RajasInsight

www.facebook.com/CreativeTalentsUnleashed

Love, A Four Letter Word Contributions:

~ Robert Ebi ~

Introducing Robert Ebi

Robert Ebi is a poet and playwright. He was born on the 6th of February. The lord of ink as he is known is famous for his style and pattern of writing. Some of his works has been published in local and international magazines.

Robert can be reached at:

https://www.facebook.com/ebi.pokey

http://www.ebirobert.blogspot.com

Love, A Four Letter Word Contributions:

Introducing Ronald Ssekajja

I am a writer from Uganda Kampala, Writing mostly Poetry and a little fiction. I have done this for the last 10 years, with two novels and 6 poetry collection (not published)
I have been having mostly on line publication for my poetry where I have received some recognitions. I am a business consultant for procurement, Marketing and Strategy.

Ronald can be reached at:

https://www.facebook.com/RonaldKSsekajja

http://www.poemhunter.com/ronald-k-ssekajja/

Love, A Four Letter Word Contributions:

Introducing Rusty Shuping

Russell "Rusty" Shuping Born 1955 in North Carolina and continues to live there. He has studied Creative Writing at RCCC, Salisbury, NC. His current writing initiative is an Action/Adventure novel. In the Past Rusty has done volunteer work including doing safe drinking water development in parts of Burkina Faso, Kenya, and Peru. He is a Independent distributor with Send Out Cards and marketing manager for Shuping Travel Service.

Rusty can be reached at:

www.facebook.com/rusty.shuping

http://shupingtravelmissions.wordpress.com/

Love, A Four Letter Word Contributions:

Introducing Siphumle Botya

I'm Siphumle Botya a young poet of 21 years of age. I became proud to call myself a poet at the age of 19 since then I haven't looked back. I'm a student nurse and I'm very passionate about helping souls into finding their way back to health. Not only am I a poet but I also love to dance.

Siphumle can be reached at:

www.facebook.com/sbotya1

http://botyasiphumle.wordpress.com

Love, A Four Letter Word Contributions:

Introducing Sreejith Kulaparambil

My full name is Sreejith Kulaparambil. By profession I am a Marketing person, but I have a deep passion for creative works and hence I do write when I get time and I even sketch and draw though nothing pursued professionally. I am very romantic from heart and very emotional too which reflects in many of my poems. I am sincerely seeking your earnest comments on my work and you can mail me your responses to email: sreejith.kulaparambil@gmail.com

Sreejith can be reached at:

www.facebook.com/sreejith.kulaparambil

www.myecstasyforyou.blogspot.com

Love, A Four Letter Word Contributions:

Introducing Stephanie Francis

Stephanie Francis is a native of Los Angeles, CA and enjoys reading, drawing, writing poetry and watching old classic films.

Stephanie can be reached at:

www.facebook.com/stephaniefran

Love, A Four Letter Word Contributions:

Introducing Steven Fortune

I wrote my first poem in 1997 while studying to obtain my BA in Literature. In the process, I would also serve as News Editor of the campus newspaper, and Editor-In-Chief of the English Department's literary arts journal. In addition, I was a contributor to the Arts Department's newsletter. In 2012, I finally broke through in the publication world, and my poetry has appeared in several journals and magazines since. I was recently named a Poetry Editor for Miracle E-Zine (though we're in the process of converting to print issues), one of the publications in which I've appeared.

Steven can be reached at:

www.facebook.com/steven.fortune.56

Love, A Four Letter Word Contributions:

Introducing Sue Lobo

Born in the UK, bought up in Botswana & South Africa as a child & now lives in Spain. Sue has two books published & has contributed to various anthologies.

Sue may be reached at:

www.facebook.com/sue.lobo.5

Love, A Four Letter Word Contributions:

~ Sunil Algama ~

Introducing Sunil Algama

I am Sunil Algama, a poet, translator and a writer from Srilanka. I am the admin of two FB groups, "English Writers" and English Poets"

https://www.facebook.com/groups/English.Writers/

https://www.facebook.com/groups/English.Poets/

Sunil can be reached at:

http://www.english-writers.com/poems.

http://poems-english.blogspot.com/

Love, A Four Letter Word Contributions:

Introducing Tony Roberts

I am a 53 year old veteran with left leg amputation. I have had 54 surgeries, and some of my hospital stays were very extensive. I had to find an escape from my loneliness, and sadness, so I spent many hours putting my heart into words.

Tony can be reached at:

www.facebook.com/tony.roberts.10048379

Love, A Four Letter Word Contributions:

Friendship   **48**

Loves Tree   **68**

Special Words   **47**

Introducing Zadok Kwame Gyesi

Zadok Kwame Gyesi is a Ghanaian poet, playwright, short story writer and a journalist. He is a product of both Mando secondary school and Ghana institute of journalism. Zadok's story themes cut across issues of culture, religion, love and crime. He is currently living in Accra working as a news reporter and editor. He has plans of travelling to UK to pursue a graduate study in creative writing.

Zadok can be reached at:

Email: zadokgee89@yahoo.com

www.zadnews.blogspot.com

www.facebook.com/zadok.kwamegyesi

Love, A Four Letter Word Contributions:

Creative Talents Unleashed

www.ctupublishinggroup.com

Join us at:

Creative

Talents

Unleashed

For writing prompts, challenges, tips and more.

www.facebook.com/Creativetalentsunleashed

www.ingramcontent.com/pod-product-compliance
Lightning Source LLC
Chambersburg PA
CBHW061731020426
42331CB00006B/1191